CLAYDON HOUSE

Buckinghamshire

National
Trust

Acknowledgements

The author is grateful to the late Sir Ralph Verney, Bt,
Sir Edmund Verney Bt, and the Trustees of the Claydon
House Trust, for access to the family papers and for help
in other ways, and to Mrs Susan Ranson, the Archivist at
Claydon, for her advice and guidance. The author is also
indebted to the previous guidebook to Claydon House
and to Dr John Broad's unpublished Ms account into
the life of the 2nd Earl Verney. Jonathan Marsden,
Anthea Palmer and Christopher Wall have kindly read
and commented upon my manuscript, and Kevin Rogers
and Jane Evans helped with the research. Philip King
and Nigel Benford, the Custodian and House Steward at
Claydon, have also been unfailingly helpful.

Tim Knox, 2002

Photographs: British Museum p. 25 (bottom left);
Courtauld Institute of Art p. 38; Sir Paul Getty KBE,
Wormsley Library p. 9 (bottom); National Gallery,
London p. 43; National Portrait Gallery, London p. 42;
National Trust pp. 8, 18, 24, 27, 30, 35, 40 (bottom), 46;
National Trust/Vera Collingwood pp. 9 (top);
National Trust Images pp. 12, 41; NT Images/Andrew
Butler p. 11; NT Images/Chris Coe p. 34; NT Images/John
Bethell pp. 3, 48, back cover; NT Images/Andreas von
Einsiedel pp. 5, 7, 10, 14, 16, 17, 20, 21, 23, 25 (top left and
right), 26, 28, 29, 32, 33, back cover; NT Images/John
Hammond pp. 1, 4, 19, 36, 37, 39, 40 (top), 45, 47 (left and
right); NT Images/John Miller front cover; Board of
Trustees of the Victoria & Albert Museum pp. 13, 31.

First published in Great Britain in 1999 by the
National Trust

© 1999 The National Trust
Registered charity no. 205846
ISBN 978-1-84359-025-5
Reprinted 2001, 2004, 2007, 2009; revised 2002, 2011, 2018

Designed by James Shurmer

Printed by Park Lane Press for National Trust (Enterprises)
Ltd, Heelis, Kemble Drive, Swindon, Wilts SN2 2NA
on Cocoon Silk made from 100% recycled paper

(Front cover) A view of Claydon from across the lake

(Title-page) Cartouche bearing the Verney coat of arms
quartered in the Servants' Hall

(Back cover) The staircase in the Hall

(Opposite) Plasterwork in the Staircase Hall

CONTENTS

LIVING AT CLAYDON

In 1936 on my 21st birthday my father gave me the Claydon estate with an empty house, one arable field and 600 acres of derelict woods.

The house was rented for a few summer weeks by an American lady, Mrs Cutting, who claimed to meet Sir Edmund Verney's ghost regularly in the first-floor passage; the rented farms had a job to earn £1 an acre; the Home Farm of 120 acres milked 20 cows; the Park was let by auction for seasonal grazing; and the woods produced bean sticks, bluebells and rabbits for the foxes of the Bicester Hunt. Then, with storm clouds gathering again in Europe, we were ordered to plough up our pastures and I gave an option to the Hall School, Hampstead, to move to Claydon in the event of war. On 3 September they arrived at 48 hours' notice, at the same time as the Army arrived to requisition the house. The Hall School remained through the freezing winter of 1939, misjudged the phoney war and returned to Hampstead in the spring of 1940 in time to be bombed: they did not return, but in the spring of 1990 we planted a cedar tree in the Church Park to commemorate their sojourn. In 1944, to escape from bomb alley, the hundred girls of West Heath School, Sevenoaks, took up residence here under their delightful Headmistress, Phyllis Elliot.

I landed at Liverpool on Grand National Day 1946 in a snowstorm and my tropical uniform, and came home to an even more derelict house, where no repairs had been possible throughout the war. I moved in with my officers' mess cook and his wife, and as the politicians like to describe it, 'took stock'. The summer of 1946 was a particularly lovely one: we finished a record haymaking before the Royal Show, and from the top of the tower, which had been a Dad's Army observation post in the war, while the cellars were filled with thousands of tins of Carnation Milk for the Ministry of Supply, my Oxford tutor, Dunstan Skilbeck, and I surveyed my inheritance and discussed how it could possibly be maintained. Then a wonderful thing happened: my darling, courageous wife agreed in 1948 to share the burden and everything became possible.

As High Sheriff of Buckinghamshire we entertained the Assize Judges in the beflagged North Hall, and instead of a Shrieval Garden Party we

A carved doorcase in the Chinese Room

(Opposite) Present-day members of the Verney family appear in eighteenth-century dress on the harpsichord painted by John Verney (John Verney Room)

gave the county a champagne concert of piano trios in the Saloon – the start of the Claydon Concerts, which over the last 33 years have delighted more than 50,000 people with over 200 concerts of exquisite music in a perfect setting, latterly with the assistance of the National Trust.

But we could not ignore the fact that the lead on our roof was becoming more and more a sieve – tin and china baths were less and less able to contain the raindrops – you could smell the mushrooms even through tobacco smoke in the Tower, and one day looking up at the dome of the Grand Stairs we saw mushrooms growing down as well as up, while little worm casts littered the floor in the Chinese Room. Our friend, relative and architect, Hugh Creighton, said we must call in the Historic Buildings Council, and the experts started to arrive and shake their heads, under the leadership of Lord Esher, who was endlessly helpful. Robin Fedden and Carew Wallace and Bobby Gore and Jim Lees-Milne all came to assess the importance of Claydon, the lawyers got busy with a Memorandum of Wishes and the HBC finally agreed to provide a substantial grant for the roof, which worked out as almost the same sum which the Trust considered acceptable for an endowment.

Over the three and a half centuries since Edmund Verney redeemed the lease of Claydon to the Giffard family in the 1620s and resumed his title as Lord of the Manor of Middle Claydon, the relationship between Claydon and Stowe was always one of competition and rivalry. Both families were deeply involved in the affairs of the Stuart court, the administration of Buckinghamshire and most of all as knights of the shire in every Parliament from James I's accession to 1918.

It is an abiding joy to me, because I was for twenty years the Chairman, on behalf of the Governors, of the Stowe Landscape Committee, that both the Stowe landscape and Claydon House now enjoy the benign and inalienable stewardship of the National Trust. This should mean not only an end of the rivalry, but also as secure and aesthetically sensitive a future as it is possible to find in our overcrowded island.

Sir RALPH VERNEY, 5TH BT, KBE, JP, DL, HON. FRIBA (1915–2001)

CLAYDON HOUSE

No more let Egypt's Pyramids Surprize
That crowd a Province & insult ye Skies
No more his Walls ye proud Assyrian boast
Raised by ye labours of a countless Host ...
One mighty fabric raised by Verney's Hands
Transcends Encomium & unrivall'd stands.

Rev. Samuel Rogers, *To Earl Verney on his magnificent seat at Claydon, Bucks* (1782)

Claydon House lies in its park amidst the lush farmland of north-west Buckinghamshire, encircled by a clutch of satellite villages which bear the picturesque names of Middle Claydon, East Claydon, Botolph Claydon and Steeple Claydon. Claydon has been the seat of the Verney family since 1620 and was home to Sir Edmund Verney, the brave 'Standard Bearer' to Charles I, and his family, whose travails during the Civil War are touchingly chronicled in *Memoirs of the Verney Family*. But the present Claydon House is almost entirely eighteenth-century, for between 1757 and 1771 it was rebuilt on a grand scale by Ralph, 2nd Earl Verney. Lord Verney wanted his house to rival nearby Stowe in magnificence, and it took the form of a great domed rotunda, flanked by two seven-bay wings – one containing the state rooms, the other a vast ballroom. At first the work was entrusted to Luke Lightfoot, a carver of genius who carried out much of the extravagant Rococo decoration of the interior, but from 1768 he was supplanted by Sir Thomas Robinson, a gentleman-architect who brought in Joseph Rose to execute Neo-classical plasterwork within the house. But Lord Verney was never to enjoy his creation, as financial ruin, brought about by his reckless extravagance, forced the sale of most of its contents in 1783 and 1784. Today, only a fragment of the great house remains, for, on the Earl's death in 1791, two-thirds of it – including the Rotunda and

the Ballroom – was demolished by his disapproving niece. Nevertheless the state rooms in the surviving wing remain some of the most magnificent and extraordinary interiors of the eighteenth century.

In the nineteenth century Claydon was inherited by the Calverts, who changed their name to Verney in accordance with the wishes of the last of the Verney line. The house enjoyed a revival under Sir Harry Verney, 2nd Bt, who extensively repaired the fabric and refurnished it in the eclectic taste of the day, introducing exotic curiosities like the Javanese gamelan, which remains one of the great surprises of Claydon. Sir Harry was devoted to his sister-in-law, Florence Nightingale, and the bedroom which she used on her frequent visits to Claydon can still be seen, together with many of her letters and other mementoes. The crowded arrangements seen in late nineteenth-century photographs of the interiors at Claydon were considerably thinned out in a sale of furniture and miscellaneous contents held in 1954, but many of the most important pieces, and the surviving family portraits, remain at Claydon.

In 1956 Claydon House was given to the National Trust which carefully restored it, bringing in John Fowler, the noted interior decorator, to advise on the redecoration of the state rooms in 1956–7 and again in 1976. Sir Edmund Verney, 6th Baronet, now lives in the east wing with his family and farms the surrounding estate.

The view from the Library through the Saloon to the North Hall gives an idea of the scale of the 2nd Earl's house, which was originally 256 feet long

THE BUILDING OF THE HOUSE

Claydon House was built by Luke Lightfoot, the brilliant stonemason and woodcarver who carried out much of the extraordinary carved decoration which is found inside it. According to Lord Verney's own account, Lightfoot was first engaged in 1757, to supply chimneypieces for Verney's town house in Curzon Street, but had quickly made himself indispensable in other ways, persuading his noble patron to entrust him with all the work at Claydon, including the drawing up of surveys and plans, the purchase of building materials, and the payment of craftsmen and labourers. But Lightfoot was not a professional architect, and indeed Verney's lack of one at Claydon was deplored by a visitor in 1768, who noted that 'a carver, one Lightfoot, is the chief man, and he seems to think of nothing but to crowd the rooms with as much carving as can be, and this in a wretched taste both in design and execution'. Although Lightfoot certainly built the house, he probably did so to someone else's design, as the restrained architectural character of the exterior is so unlike the extravagant decorations he devised for the interior. The Rev. Samuel Rogers, in a footnote to his poem *To Earl Verney on his magnificent seat at Claydon, Bucks* (1782), claimed that 'In this stupendous work Earl Verney was his own architect', and his assertion should not be totally discounted. As a cultivated nobleman who is known to have been interested in architecture and building, Verney could well have designed his own house, doubtless with some discreet professional help.

Although the surviving range was at first probably intended as a complete house in its own right (a mid-eighteenth-century design drawing of the west front shows it with a door in the place of the central Venetian window), as it is today, Claydon House is but a fragment of a much larger house. Such was the 2nd Earl's taste for grandeur and

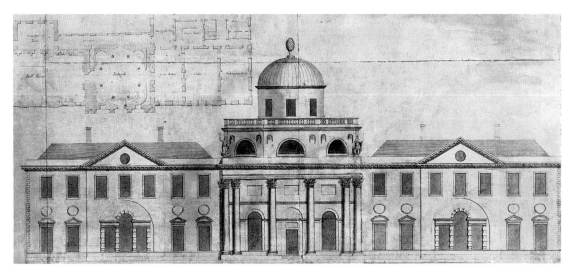

Sir Thomas Robinson's design for the west front; only the right-hand wing survives (Paper Room)

lavish entertainments that he greatly extended it by an immense addition to the north, which almost trebled the length of the principal front and made the existing house merely the southern-most wing or pavilion of a great palace. The work began in 1768, just as the earlier phase of construction was drawing to a close, and chiefly consisted of two huge reception rooms, a circular entrance hall or rotunda and a ballroom. The full extent of these additions – which were demolished in 1791–2, scarcely twenty years after they were built – are shown in a pen-and-wash elevation which hangs in the Paper Room, and in a recently discovered watercolour view of 1773 (illustrated below).

The west front today

Standing before the west front of the present house, one must imagine a second, duplicate, building far to the left. Behind its façade lay a single immense room, a columned Ballroom or 'Egyptian Hall', seven bays long and two storeys high. Giving off it to the east was a smaller 'Withdrawing Room'. Between the two wings, roughly on the site of the present gravelled area before the north front, was the noble Rotunda, expressed on the outside of the house by six giant engaged Corinthian columns, with the front door in the centre. According to the county historian George Lipscomb, the Rotunda took the form of 'a saloon, comprising fifty feet, containing a circle of lofty columns of artificial jasper with white marble bases and capitals, supporting an entablature and gallery, with an iron balustrade ... crowned with a dome'. Above, a domed cupola

with a gilt pineapple on its summit, topped 'a circular belvedere, from the windows of which there were very beautiful views of the surrounding country to a great distance, extending to the Welsh mountains' – the latter possibly achieved by the 'very large reflecting telescope on a mahogany stand, by Nairn', sold from the room in 1783. After this extension, the façade of the house was some 256 feet long, and rivalled nearby Stowe as the most splendid seat in the county, but it must have always looked rather like two country houses linked by a rotunda, clearly betraying its origins as an extravagant afterthought added to the original seven-bay range.

For his spectacular work of aggrandisement, Verney clearly required an architectural mentor

The 2nd Earl's mansion from the park in 1773 (Private Collection)

and he found one in Sir Thomas Robinson, a Yorkshire baronet and an amateur architect, who, on his return from an unpopular term as Governor of Barbados, acquired a controlling interest in the celebrated pleasure gardens at Ranelagh in Chelsea and became its Master of Ceremonies. Verney probably knew Robinson through Ranelagh, as he had been persuaded to invest heavily in the venture, but he also sought his advice on matters of architecture. The baronet, a rather conventional architect of the Burlingtonian-Palladian school, had rebuilt his own house at Rokeby Hall in Yorkshire and been extensively employed at Castle Howard. He is known to have advised on the design of the extended west front at Claydon, and his letters make particular reference to the Rotunda – it is tempting to speculate whether the circular central feature of Lord Verney's house was inspired by the great Rotunda which formed the principal attraction at Ranelagh. The extended Claydon also bore a marked resemblance to Prospect Place, Robinson's own house at

Ranelagh, which also took the form of a rotunda flanked by wings. But much of Sir Thomas's work was practical, for he sought to correct the alarming signs of structural weakness which bedevilled the shell and roof of the Ballroom during construction – problems which he claimed were a consequence of Lightfoot's 'total ignorance of carrying on work, or designing with propriety'. Even more serious was Robinson's discovery that Lightfoot had been systematically overcharging and defrauding his patron. It was on his recommendation that Joseph Rose was brought in to carry out plasterwork in the completed portion of the house, an imposition which, not surprisingly, Lightfoot resented, and he retaliated by becoming increasingly dilatory and unco-operative. Lightfoot was eventually dismissed in August 1769.

After Lightfoot's departure, Robinson strove to solve the structural problems that beset the new wing and complete its half-finished decorations, but he and Verney themselves quarrelled in 1771. From then on, the finishing of the interior progressed fitfully, because of Verney's increasingly precarious finances, under the direction of the former Clerk of Works, a minor but proficient architect called William Donn. But in 1784 work came to an abrupt halt as financial ruin engulfed the 2nd Earl, forcing the sale of his furniture and his flight to France. For years the house stood empty, and it is little wonder that, on inheriting Claydon on the death of the 2nd Earl in 1791, his niece, Mary, Baroness Fermanagh, ordered the demolition of the Rotunda and Ballroom. The work of demolishing these huge and impractical additions was carried out by a 'Mr Leverton', who may be Thomas Leverton, the London architect and builder. The materials were carefully salvaged and sold, or reused elsewhere on the estate – the stone fronts of the estate cottages facing into the park come from the demolished house. Today no trace remains of Lord Verney's Ballroom and Rotunda, and indeed doubts were at one time expressed if they were actually ever built at all. However, archaeological investigations recently carried out in the forecourt have revealed tantalising sections of their foundations lurking beneath the gravel.

This ornately carved door (now shown in the Paper Room) may have been designed for the east wing, but was probably never installed

TOUR OF THE HOUSE

The Exterior

THE NORTH FRONT

The visitor arrives at Claydon before the north front of the house, a severe façade of grey cut stone pierced with five bays of windows. It looks like the side wall of the house and is indeed just that, for it was largely erected in 1791–2 to hide the scar made by the demolition of the great Rotunda, the entrance hall of the 2nd Earl's gigantic house, which occupied the site of the present forecourt.

The demolition of the Rotunda deprived Claydon of its front door, and until 1862 visitors entered the house via a modest doorway in the brick east range, to the left of the present entrance. In that year Sir Harry Verney, 2nd Bt had the sills of two of the ground-floor windows lowered and made them into doors. The lack of a central doorway clearly displeased Sir Harry, and he intended to disguise this by erecting in front of them a carriage porch befitting the size and dignity of the house, adorned with two huge native 'idols', which had been obtained by his eldest son in Canada. Alas, Sir Harry's bizarre *porte-cochère* never came to pass.

THE EAST WING

The large brick range which extends out from the house on the left is the east wing, containing the family and service apartments. Built on the site of the Jacobean manor house and containing much seventeenth-century fabric, it was begun around 1757, but was extensively recast in 1859–62 for the

The west front

2nd Baronet. It is still the residence of the members of the Verney family who live at Claydon. Further east is the Stable Court in diapered brick, built by the 2nd Earl and helpfully dated 1754, the first of his improvements at Claydon. To the right a gate leads on to the lawn before the west front, the former entrance façade of the house.

THE WEST FRONT

The principal ornamental front of Claydon House overlooks the park and is a handsome but unostentatious seven-bay range of cut stone. The three projecting middle bays bear a pediment, and in the centre of the façade, recessed within a shallow niche, is a large Venetian window, its central arch and vertical elements defined by projecting blocks of masonry. The other windows on the ground floor are crowned with pedimented entablatures, and above each is a bull's-eye window which also lights the apartments on the ground floor, hinting at the loftiness of the state rooms within. The 2nd Earl Verney probably embarked on the construction of this part of his house only after the completion of the south, or family, wing which lies behind it. The portion at the back containing the Pink Parlour and the Staircase Hall was well advanced by 1759, and the three state rooms along the west front were being decorated in 1768.

The North Hall in 1893

The Interior

THE NORTH HALL

Since 1862 this lofty room has served as the Entrance Hall, but it was once the Great Eating Room of the 2nd Earl's magnificent house. It originally gave off the circular Rotunda, which stood beyond the wall opposite the fireplace. It is a double cube, 50 feet long, 25 feet wide and 25 feet high, and the explosion of Lightfoot's carved woodwork which greets the visitor makes for a worthy introduction to his work elsewhere in the house.

CEILING

The ceiling is divided into three compartments: the central division is filled by a great boss of writhing foliage for the chandelier with the Verney phoenix crest on either side; the outer bays have sunburst-like trophies of militaria – muskets, battleaxes, spears, cannon, etc. – marshalled by three hovering putti. The surrounding cartouches contain the 2nd Earl's coronet and cipher, 'RV'. Unusually, all this decoration is of carved wood rather than plaster. Only the frieze, with medallion busts of Apollo and Clytie in each of the circular metopes, is of plaster.

DOORCASES AND NICHES

The doorcases and the surrounds to the niches are also carved in wood. With its exhilarating combination of shell-like curves and flourishes of foliage, infested with human heads, fantastic ho-ho birds and monsters, the woodwork is an extreme example of the Rococo decoration, a taste which enjoyed a tremendous vogue throughout Europe in the mid-eighteenth century and which was widely disseminated by engraved designs in pattern books. Indeed it is thought that Lightfoot based his carvings on such engravings, particularly the plates depicting designs for wall-lights and looking-glasses published by Matthias Lock in 1744. The catalogue of the 1784 sale of Earl Verney's furniture tells us that each niche once contained 'an elegant marble bust' representing the continents of Africa, Asia, Europe and America. The present busts are casts of an eighteenth-century Italian set

Lightfoot's Rococo carvings in the North Hall were probably based on engravings from Matthias Lock's Six Sconces *(1744)*

of the continents, attributed to the Neapolitan sculptor Lorenzo Vacaro, c.1690 although they may be Genoese. The originals belong to the Compton Verney House Trust (Peter Moores Foundation).

Lightfoot appears to have visited Claydon only infrequently and carved the decoration of the room in his Southwark workshop. However, it must have been at least partly installed by the autumn of 1769, for on 9 September Sir Thomas Robinson wrote to Earl Verney expressing his horror at the capricious taste of its ornaments:

Mr Lightfoot's design for finishing the great eating Room shock'd me so much and is so much the ridicule of all that have seen or heard of it, & which when done, yr Ldp will undo – that it would be the want of that Friendship I profess to yr Ldp not to acquaint you thereof – & therefore I will undertake to do it on a different design, in some measure parallel to & proper to the Work of the Hall & Ball Room … all this may be done … *at an easier Expense* than it will cost you ever to finish what he has begun – & if done by him will indeed be what he expresses very justly – *such a Work as the World never saw.*

Lightfoot was dismissed in the following year, but fortunately Verney resisted his architect's entreaties, and Lightfoot's decoration survives, although the great doorcase opposite the chimney-piece, which is in a 'correct' taste and was once the entrance to the Ballroom, may be by Robinson. However, its extraordinary pediment with snake-necked ho-ho birds is certainly the work of Lightfoot, although it may not always have been intended for this position. In 1893, grained to resemble mahogany, the birds formed the cresting of a sideboard in the room.

CHIMNEYPIECE

The chimneypiece has ornaments of white marble which were probably carved in Lightfoot's work-shop, set off by Sicilian jasper and yellow sienna marble. Its frieze is supported by composite columns assisted by Bacchic camp-followers. Both bear baskets of grapes on their heads, an allusion to the original function of the room, and on the central tablet is a Verney phoenix. The awkward way in which some of these elements fit together

The elaborate chimney-piece, overmantel carvings and niches in the North Hall were all the work of Luke Lightfoot and his workshop

suggests that the chimneypiece may have been put together by another sculptor out of the unfinished or unassembled carvings which we know were seized from Lightfoot's workshop after his fall from grace in 1769. The sculptor Robert Chambers was employed in 1779–82 making designs for such hybrid confections, including a chimneypiece incorporating 'two marble cariatides already executed', one holding a lyre, the other a guitar, now sadly lost. The pair of swans which flanks the balustraded bridge in the lower part of the wooden overmantel probably symbolises the nearby county town of Buckingham, the object of Earl Verney's expensive political ambitions. The carvings higher up may have originally belonged elsewhere and been fixed here only at a later date – the boy-headed brackets probably began life in a chimneypiece.

DECORATION

In the late nineteenth century, the walls became increasingly cluttered with regimental flags, antlers and Asiatic weaponry. The present decorative scheme with subtle shades of lemon yellow and green was devised by John Fowler in 1956–7, and the room was redecorated again under his supervision in 1976. Fowler's work at Claydon is one of the most successful of his collaborations with the National Trust and provides an effective foil for its remarkable eighteenth-century architecture and decoration.

MODEL

The model shows Claydon House as it was in c.1784. It was made in 1999–2000 by George Rome Innes.

THE SALOON

Although it was also fitted up under Lightfoot's direction, the Saloon, with its plaster coffering, rich Venetian window and columned, tabernacle-like doorcases, presents an almost conventional picture of Palladian splendour after the unbridled display of Rococo in the North Hall. Even Lightfoot's great critic, Sir Thomas Robinson, had to admit that 'the saloon and Drawing Room [now

the Library] ... are not so bad, & their absurdities might be easily remedied'. Well he might, for the ceiling is probably by Joseph Rose the Younger, whom Robinson had himself recommended in 1768 as 'the first man in the Kingdom as a Plaisterrer'.

CEILING

Rose carried out Neo-classical stucco decoration in other rooms at Claydon and was later to be extensively employed by Robert Adam at Osterley and elsewhere. Robinson says he was assisted at Claydon by two workmen named 'Petroles and Couldock ... the best of his men'. The first of these, Petrolli or Patroli, is recorded by Lipscomb as being 'an Italian artist of great ingenuity, long employed here' and credited with the design and execution of a relief representing *Venus supported by Bacchus and Ceres*, once in the centre of the Ballroom ceiling. The coving, with its perspectival coffering and the cartouche containing an ideal female head, is all of plaster, but the frieze and outer band of ceiling decoration are made of papier mâché.

CHIMNEYPIECE

The rich doorcases, window surround, dado rail and skirtings are all carved in wood, but they are eclipsed in magnificence by the massive sculptured chimneypiece, which tells the story of the invention of the Corinthian order, as described by Vitruvius, the ancient authority on classical architecture. The female figure, perhaps the grieving nurse of the young Corinthian maiden in the legend, clutches the basket she left on the girl's grave. Around it has grown up an acanthus plant, which, according to Vitruvius, was the inspiration of the Corinthian capital – an order splendidly illustrated in the surround of the Venetian window of the room. Her male counterpart is its inventor, the youthful architect Callimachus, holding a pair of dividers and a broken column-base, respectively the symbols of his craft and the girl's untimely death. In the inner frieze carved putti glumly gambol amidst flowers and berries, one holds a tragic mask, another a basket, while in the centre is a medallion portrait of the dead maiden,

which the putti mournfully crown with a funereal wreath. The chimneypiece is often attributed, on scanty evidence, to the sculptor Thomas Carter the Younger, but the pedestal figures closely resemble those on the North Hall chimneypiece, which were almost certainly carved in Lightfoot's workshop. However, the superb frieze of putti is clearly the work of a different hand and bears a strong affinity with work by Thomas Carter's uncle, Benjamin, who died in 1766, and it may be that this is a joint effort. As with the chimneypiece in the North Hall, a certain clumsiness in its makeup suggests that the carvings were assembled by another hand, perhaps the sculptor Robert Chambers.

DOORS

The mahogany doors are particularly notable, with their raised shell-like mouldings and inlays of ebony and boxwood, the corners set with ivory cinquefoils.

DECORATION

The present decoration and arrangement of the room dates from 1957, when the walls were hung with a grey-blue flock copied from a mid-Georgian paper found at Lydiard Tregoze in Wiltshire. In 1976 its fading colour was refreshed by spraying with blue paint.

FURNITURE

In the 1783 sale the Saloon lost its magnificent suite of mahogany seat furniture comprising twelve elbow chairs and two sofas all 'stuft and covered with blue silk and worsted damask', as well as 'a large pier glass in oval plates ... richly carved and gilt in burnished gold ornamented with trophies of dogs, birds &c'. However, by the late nineteenth century, photographs show that these losses had been somewhat overcompensated for by the introduction of an enormous quantity of miscellaneous furniture. This included the set

(Left)
The ceiling plasterwork in the Saloon was carried out by Joseph Rose

(Right)
The Saloon chimneypiece illustrates the legend of the invention of the Corinthian order

The Saloon in 1893

of chairs covered in *gros point* embroidery which remains in the room, each one worked by various friends of the Verney family in the 1850s. The end wall was once dominated by a great glazed cabinet made out of Brazilian kaya-buca wood, containing a collection of stuffed South American birds, but after 1898 its place was taken by a monster chamber organ, which is now in a church in Coventry.

PICTURES

The walls are hung with some of the best family portraits in the house. In pride of place above the chimneypiece hangs a Van Dyck studio portrait of Charles I in a magnificent 'auricular' frame, flanked by likenesses of Sir Ralph Verney,

1st Bt, by Lely, and his wife Mary, after Van Dyck, and of the mysterious Colonel and Mrs Herbert, the latter by J. M. Wright. On the opposite wall is Van Dyck's Sir Edmund Verney, the 'Standard Bearer' flanked by Lady Anne Herbert, the Countess of Carnarvon after Van Dyck, and a Mytens-like portrait said to be of Sir Francis Verney (1584–1616), Sir Edmund's scapegrace half-brother, who became a pirate and came to a sorry end in Messina, but more probably of Sir Edmund himself, painted around 1625. The actual canes held by Sir Edmund and 'Sir Francis' are suspended below their portraits. Between the doors on the wall opposite the windows, hangs an interesting icon-like portrait of Charles I as Prince of Wales. It is a reduced copy of a portrait attributed to Paul van Somer now in Copenhagen.

THE LIBRARY

The third of the great state rooms that lie behind the west front, the Library is a double cube of the same dimensions as the North Hall. It was originally called the 'Withdrawing Room' or the 'Blue Drawing Room' and had furniture upholstered in 'rich blue silk and worsted damask'.

CEILING

The Neo-classical plasterwork of the ceiling is similar in spirit to that in the Saloon and must be another work of Joseph Rose and his team – in July 1768 Sir Thomas Robinson reported that Rose would 'finish the Staircase and the two ceilings by Xmas' and he was doubtless referring to these two rooms. As in the Saloon, the frieze is of papier mâché, but the preposterous wooden brackets in the form of winged putti heads springing from flowers and acanthus are doubtless by Lightfoot.

DOORCASES AND WINDOW SURROUNDS

The handsome doorcases and garlanded window surrounds are in a rich Neo-classical taste and were perhaps installed by the architect William Donn, a disciple of Robert Adam, who took over the finishing of the house after Robinson's departure in 1771.

CHIMNEYPIECE

The chimneypiece is a comparatively staid eighteenth-century affair in white statuary and sienna marbles on a ground of red Languedoc marble, supported by figures of Apollo and Diana, emblematic of the sun and the moon and the patrons respectively of the Arts and hunting. It was perhaps

A nineteenth-century watercolour of the Library

brought here from elsewhere in the house, as the original chimneypiece is said to have been seized by the 2nd Earl's creditors.

BOOKCASES

The Library was converted to its present use by Parthenope, the second wife of Sir Harry Verney, 2nd Bt, in 1861–2, using bookshelves brought here from a library in the east wing, which had been divided up into bedrooms in 1859. The old shelving was extended by the provision of corner cupboards and garnished with eighteenth-century carvings found in the cellars and outhouses. The pierced console brackets on the pilasters appear to have been brought down from the cornice of the Paper Room upstairs. In August 1862 Lady Verney proudly wrote to her stepson, 'I cannot tell you how the bookcases are admired ... all say there is nothing better in the Exhibition [the London International Exhibition of 1862]'.

DECORATION

Throughout much of the nineteenth century the Library was painted green, although it 'had faded to a very bilious colour' by 1912 and was replaced by red. The walls are now painted blue.

SCULPTURE

The alcove contains a bronze statue of Parthenope's famous younger sister, Florence Nightingale, by their cousin Hilary Bonham-Carter.

PICTURES

Fittingly, over the chimneypiece, Sir William Blake Richmond's portrait of Lady Verney, 1869, presides over her creation; his portrait of her husband hangs in the middle of the far wall. A series of portraits of members of the Calvert family hangs above the bookshelves and doorcases.

FURNITURE

The Library is now rather more densely furnished than the other rooms at Claydon and contains a superb Wilton carpet bought for £100 at the Great Exhibition in 1851.

The octagonal micro-mosaic tabletop (see illustration p. 47) with a head of Silenus in the centre

The carved balusters on the Library steps may have come from a staircase designed by Lightfoot once in the much-remodelled south wing

is signed by 'C Ciuli F.A. 1825' and was among the many works of art bought in Rome in the winter of 1826–7 by Lord Western for his house, Felix Hall in Essex. It arrived in England 'broken into fragments' and was given to Sir Harry by its owner. He had it repaired and mounted on its base, which is made up, as is usual at Claydon, of carvings by Lightfoot from the demolished portion of the house.

Another example of this reuse of carved woodwork is the set of library steps, which was made for Parthenope, Lady Verney, in about 1860, and incorporates five Rococo staircase balusters, each of a different design. This, and another pair supporting a lectern in the Library, may be by

Lightfoot and may come from a subsidiary staircase once in the south wing, dismantled during the alterations in 1859.

BOOKS

The books are a miscellaneous family collection reflecting the tastes and enthusiasms of successive generations of the Verneys, being particularly well stocked with works on theology, agricultural improvement and travel.

A short service corridor leads to the Staircase Hall.

THE STAIRCASE OR BLACK AND WHITE HALL

The staircase occupies a majestic domed compartment, known by the family as the 'Black and White Hall', which rises the full height of the house, its walls covered with elegant trophies and festoons in stucco, occupied by a staircase of unrivalled richness, inlaid with exotic woods and ivory, and railed by a wrought-iron balustrade of remarkable virtuosity.

Although the staircase was well advanced by the summer of 1768, Lightfoot's role in the progress of this *tour de force* of eighteenth-century craftsmanship predictably caused Sir Thomas Robinson considerable disquiet. In July 1768 Robinson wrote to Earl Verney about the stucco decoration: 'Mr Rose has been with me ... complaining that Mr Lightfoot retarded the Staircase by not sending the instruction wanting. I beg your Ldp would write to him on this head. Mr Rose says he can finish the Staircase & the two Ceilings [those of the Saloon and Library] by Xmas, if not retarded by his Joyners.' Nevertheless even Robinson had to concede that 'the Staircase will be very Noble and Great, Mr Rose's part very beautiful indeed, & when compleated it will be one of the very great works of Claydon'. From this it is evident that

The frieze beneath the Staircase Hall skylight was carved by Lightfoot with fish-tailed putti and the figure of Neptune riding a sea-horse

Lightfoot and his workmen were entrusted with the joinery and inlay of the staircase, while Rose carried out the stucco decoration on the walls and ceiling.

WALL DECORATION

Rose's wall decoration takes the form of a continuous festoon, alternately of plaster drapery and laurel leaves, from which are suspended a variety of *trompe-l'oeil* medallions, lamps and trophies. Reliefs depicting mythological scenes fill some of the larger expanses of wall on the landings, and Earl Verney's coronet is prominently displayed lower down. Above the doors on the half-landings are charming trophies composed of a putto firmly grasping the tails of two gasping dolphins. In the redecoration of 1956, these ornaments were picked out in white on blue grounds, against walls of a pinkish biscuit colour.

CEILING

High up above the second floor is a deep coving of plaster coffering, each compartment containing a rosette or flower. Around the base of the glass skylight is a frieze, its ornaments superbly carved of wood in high relief, depicting Neptune and Thetis riding hippocamps (seahorses) upon a choppy sea, attended by fish-tailed putti. Being of wood, the carvings must be by Lightfoot and perhaps represent the portion of the decoration which Robinson wrote of in 1768 as being 'better suited to Mr Lightfoot's work'.

STAIRCASE

The staircase itself is made of mahogany and, owing to the height of the state rooms on ground level, gently ascends to the first floor in two circuits, pausing at each level with a generous landing. The tread and riser of each step are elaborately inlaid with box and ebony, the lower flights being further embellished with tiny discs of ivory. The undersides of the stairs are also inlaid, as are the doors of the room. The balustrade is of ironwork finely wrought as a continuous series of elaborate scrolls, linked by a garland of gilded husks and ears of corn. The craftsman who made the balustrade is not known, but the extreme

delicacy of its elements causes them to quiver and rub against each other when anyone ascends the stairs, and the rustling noise thus produced, together with the creaking of the marquetry, has led to a legend that the staircase 'sings'. Sadly, such is the fragility of the staircase that this curious phenomenon can no longer be experienced by visitors.

The staircase was carefully restored in 1976 and repainted by John Fowler in what he believed to be its original livery of greenish-black and gold – although family tradition staunchly asserts that the 2nd Earl Verney abhorred gilding and forbade its use in the decoration of his house. It was then that the original colours of the Verney arms on the landing were uncovered from beneath layers of overpaint. The fine inlaid handrail ends in a spectacular whorl at the foot of the stairs and below it, as if to proclaim the splendid decadence of its workmanship, the bottom step of the staircase lazily extends out into a final flourish, luxuriously inlaid with coloured woods and ivory.

Visitors now use a subsidiary staircase located within the nineteenth-century water-tower on the north-east corner of the house. The stair was built in 1957 as a gift from Sir Harry Verney, 4th Bt.

THE PINK PARLOUR

The last of the surviving ground-floor state rooms, this disproportionately lofty parlour was presumably named after its original colour, which was restored on the basis of paint scrapes in the early 1980s. In 1783 it contained a 'Square mahogany table with drawers and sliders with springs, [which] forms a writing, dressing, breakfast, chess, backgammon & draft table with men, compleat' and was probably also used for more intimate meals and entertainments – a purpose which it served right up until recent times.

DECORATION

The decoration, including the compartmented ceiling, the rich cornice and window surrounds and the doorcases, is all of carved wood and is probably the work of Luke Lightfoot and his workshop.

(Opposite) The Staircase Hall

DOORCASES

The doorcases are of particular interest, being of conventional form but with lively friezes carved with foliage, bearing tablets representing scenes from *Aesop's Fables* based on Francis Barlow's illustrations in the popular edition of 1687. The doors are of 'Spanish mahogany' from Jamaica, and are estimated to weigh half a ton each.

VENETIAN WINDOW

The east wall of the room is taken up by a large Venetian window framed by Ionic pilasters. Its unusual octagonal glazing bars perhaps derived from geometric designs for window tracery promoted in the pattern books of Batty Langley and others.

CHIMNEYPIECE

The chimneypiece surround is also of wood, the frieze carved with foliage scrolls, birds, fruiting pomegranates and a central basket of flowers, while the vertical elements bear 'drops' of grapes and vine leaves, flanked by Bacchic busts on scroll consoles, garlanded with vines. In the centre of the marble insert is the head of Apollo, emerging from a sunburst, perhaps hinting at the room's function as an informal breakfast room.

PICTURES

Above the chimneypiece, amidst the arrangement of Rococo flourishes which forms the overmantel, is a portrait of John Verney, the 1st Earl Verney's eldest son, whose premature death meant the title and estate went in 1752 to his improvident younger brother, Ralph. On the opposite wall is a full-length portrait of Margaret, Lady Verney (d. 1930), wife of the 3rd Baronet, shown standing on the stairs at Claydon, by Sir William Blake Richmond (1869). The wall to the right of the fireplace is hung with portraits of Viscount Fermanagh, the father of the 1st Earl Verney, and his three wives. The 1st Earl's portrait hangs over the door to the left of the fireplace.

A door to the right of the Venetian window leads to a staircase, by which visitors ascend to the first floor of the house.

*The Pink Parlour
about 1893*

The Stork and the Fox: the tablets over the doors in the Pink Parlour are based on Francis Barlow's illustrations for the 1687 edition of Aesop's Fables

THE GREAT RED ROOM

This is the first of three large rooms on the first floor with the curious feature of a triad of domes let into their ceilings. The Great Red Room, Paper Room and Gothic Room may originally have been intended as the principal bedrooms, the domes echoing the domed canopies over the beds.

This room may be the 'Velvet Bed Chamber' mentioned in the 1784 sale catalogue, but is described as the 'Red Parlor' in a late eighteenth-century plan, so its use as an upstairs sitting-room

Detail of the chimneypiece in the Great Red Room

was evidently established by then. Despite its name, historically it was always painted blue. A keystone, dated 1759 and inscribed with the name of a mason called James Bull, was uncovered above the east window during restoration work and this suggests that this part of the house (the Staircase Hall and the Pink Parlour below this room) was well advanced by this time.

DOME AND WINDOW DECORATION

The domes and the fretwork mouldings that surround them are all of carved wood and so must be by Lightfoot's workmen. In his letters to Lord Verney about the house, Sir Thomas Robinson seems resigned to Lightfoot retaining control of the first-floor decoration – either because it was too far advanced to halt or because he considered it relatively unimportant. Certainly Lightfoot's hand can be seen in the carved surrounds of the windows, which terminate with toothy dolphins and lion masks emerging from scrolls.

CHIMNEYPIECE

Lightfoot may also have executed the chimneypiece with supporters in the form of vine-wreathed 'maenads' (followers of Bacchus), clad in wild-animal skins, as well as the fretwork dado.

Lightfoot's window surrounds in the Great Red Room feature lion masks and dolphins

PICTURES

On the west wall hangs a full-length portrait after Sir Thomas Lawrence of William Pitt, 1st Earl Amherst, who made a celebrated embassy to China in 1816–17. The Earl was the grandfather of Margaret Hay-Williams, wife of Sir Edmund Hope Verney. Verney portraits also hang here.

From the door which opens on to the staircase landing, visitors can admire its carving and stucco decoration.

THE GARLAND CHAMBER

This narrow room may originally have been a dressing-room, and is named after the wreaths of laurel that are applied to the doors. It has door-cases with broken pediments and a chimneypiece to match, with an insert of violet breccia marble. The pediment of the chimneypiece and the tiled grate date from the late nineteenth century. Fittingly the dressing room now contains an annual exhibition drawn from Claydon's remarkable costume collection.

THE MUSEUM

The lobby at the top of the Staircase, embedded in the body of the house and lit by a tall octagonal lantern, can only have been a room of communication, as it has so many doors and no fireplace. However, it has been known as the Museum since it became home to the family collection of curiosities in 1893. In October that year Sir Harry wrote to his eldest son explaining how 'when you come you will find a great change in the Lobby outside the Chinese Room. It is now a sort of Museum and I am sure it will interest and amuse you.' Old photographs show it gloriously stuffed with ethnographic artefacts and curios, some of which still survive here, and it was especially rich in artefacts from the Haida and Tsimshian cultures of British Columbia in western Canada, collected by Edmund Hope Verney in the 1860s. Most imposing were two big Salish house posts from Comox, described by Edmund in a list of artefacts he shipped back to England in 1863 as 'two large carvings from the mouth of the Courtenay River in the Comux District'. These, he suggested, 'will

The Museum in 1902

do for garden gateposts', but his father had an even more bizarre proposal, which he described in a letter dated September 1864: 'If I can ever afford to build a Portico on the N side of this house at the Entrance Hall, under which carriages can drive to the Door, your beautiful Carvings, like Gog and Magog, may stand on each side to test the Courage of Visitors ... to terrify naughty children.' They ended up in the family museum, but were sold in 1931 and are now in the British Museum.

With its bewildering array of native clubs, corals and cork models, and cabinets stuffed with tribal masks and Greek vases, the Claydon House Museum was one of the most impressive of all country house ensembles of this kind. Although many of its contents are now dispersed, in recent years an attempt has been made to return to the room the atmosphere of a Victorian family museum. Among the exhibits are objects connected with Florence Nightingale, who, as the sister of Parthenope, Lady Verney, was a frequent guest at Claydon.

GAMELAN

The greatest treasure of the Museum is the gamelan, an orchestra of gongs and other instruments from Java, which was used to accompany religious or ceremonial rituals. It was made in the second half of the eighteenth century and reputedly comes from Gresnik, a small port a few miles north of Surabaya in eastern Java, where it was acquired in 1814 by Sir Stamford Raffles, the celebrated colonial administrator and Lieutenant Governor of Java from 1811 to 1816. Raffles brought the instrument back to England, and it was displayed at his country house, High Wood near Hendon, until Lady Raffles's death in 1858. The Claydon gamelan was bought from her heirs in 1861 by Sir Harry Verney – for a considerable sum, as Parthenope, Lady Verney, gave up her allowance for six months to enable her husband to make the purchase. Evidently made for noble, or even royal use, no other gamelan can rival it for the richness and splendour of its decoration, which most appropriately given its present setting, is derived from European Rococo sources rather than traditional Javanese motifs.

MISS NIGHTINGALE'S ROOM

This room, which corresponds to the Garland Chamber across the lobby, was where the redoubtable Florence Nightingale stayed during her frequent visits to Claydon between 1857 and 1890. It has therefore been decorated as it was in her day, with Lightfoot's fine eighteenth-century woodwork grained to resemble pale oak and a densely patterned paper on the walls. The walls are thickly hung with portraits of her and other mementoes. The sharp curves of the broken pediments above the doorcases and the chimneypiece,

Miss Nightingale's Room

The ceiling of the Gothic Room

and the long lancets of beading on the doors, are almost Gothic in flavour – as if to prepare one for the Gothic Room.

THE JOHN VERNEY ROOM

(MISS NIGHTINGALE'S DRESSING ROOM)

This small room, which was perhaps Florence Nightingale's dressing-room, contains an exhibition of the work of Sir John Verney, MC (1913–93), a talented painter and book illustrator, and a kinsman of the Verneys of Claydon. The exhibits include a harpsichord charmingly painted with a view of the south front of Claydon. The figures in eighteenth-century dress are portraits of present-day members of the Verney family, and a ho-ho bird perches in the oak tree on the lawn.

THE GOTHIC OR BLUE ROOM

Used in the 1860s as a boudoir by the ladies of the Verney household, this room was originally a bedroom, perhaps for Countess Verney. Its windows look directly on to the venerable parish church of Middle Claydon, and the view may have inspired the fanciful mock-medieval theme of its ornaments. It was perhaps the 'Blue and Silver Bed Chamber, fronting the Church' described in the 1784 sale catalogue, and if this is so, it once contained a 'mahogany bedstead with carved dome tester and headboard' hung with 'yellow mxt. damask drapery furniture' – which may explain the three octagonal domes on the ceiling.

DECORATION

Made of wood, like those in the Great Red Room, the domes are surrounded by fretwork compartments and enriched with applied carved decoration in the Gothic taste. The repeated motif

29

of a triple-arched pavilion also occurs above the doorcases and window surrounds, as well as on the central tablet of the chimneypiece. Clusters of slender columns flank the windows and doors, which are themselves inlaid with Gothic patterns in holly and boxwood. The dado is heavily carved and coffered, while the window shutters are carved with lancets filled with Gothic tracery.

CHIMNEYPIECE

The chimneypiece is of white statuary marble combined with Sicilian jasper and sienna marble and continues the prickly theme of the room.

PICTURES

Above the chimneypiece is a mixed-media portrait of Lady Lucy Calvert by Sir W. B. Richmond. The room also contains a remarkable set of six large Chinese paintings of social gatherings, done for the European market in the eighteenth century. They are not indigenous to Claydon, but were bequeathed to the National Trust by Sir Noel and Lady Charles in 1995.

The Chinese Room heaped with curios, in about 1890

The alcove in the Chinese Room would originally have contained a divan, as in this illustration from Ince and Mayhew's Universal System of Household Furniture *(1762)*

THE CHINESE ROOM

The richly decorated Chinese Room is without doubt the glory of Claydon, as well as being one of the most extraordinary rooms in any English country house. It was probably an intimate upstairs sitting-room between bedrooms – the Gothic Room and what is now the Paper Room.

ALCOVE

The alcove would have contained a day-bed or divan for taking tea and, most appropriately, it takes the form of a Chinese fretwork teahouse with overhanging eaves, trimmed with icicles, bells and exuberant Rococo decoration, its front and sides embowered by clambering vines. The niches were doubtless originally filled with oriental porcelain or curios. Inside the alcove is a frieze depicting a tea ceremony carved in startling high relief, but carved bunches of grapes suggest that stronger beverages were sometimes partaken of here.

DOORCASES AND CHIMNEYPIECES

The Chinese theme of the decoration is carried on by the doorcases, surmounted by airy bell-hung pagodas sheltering fretwork shelves for yet more porcelain and flanked by scrolled consoles bearing oriental busts. Orientals also support the two chimneypieces of the room.

CHINOISERIE

All this elaborate decoration – which is of carved wood – is by Luke Lightfoot and his workshop and is in a pronounced chinoiserie taste, a term used to express the frivolous Chinese-Rococo style of decoration that enjoyed a tremendous vogue throughout Europe in the mid-eighteenth century. Inspired by the scenes on imported porcelain and lacquer screens, and by serious publications like Sir William Chambers's *Designs of Chinese Buildings, Furniture, Dresses, etc.* (1757), the chinoiserie style playfully combined Chinese motifs with Rococo curves and scrolls, producing an essentially ephemeral style, which came to be used in architecture, interior decoration and furniture, as well as the decorative arts in every medium. The Chinese Room at Claydon is important as among the most fantastic and full-blooded examples of the chinoiserie style to survive anywhere.

SOURCES

As with the North Hall, Lightfoot probably derived his ideas from the many pattern books which appeared in the 1750s and '60s for the use of cabinetmakers and designers – works like George Edwards and Matthias Darley's *Chinese Designs* (1754) or Chippendale's *Director* of the same year. The chimneypieces, for instance, are 'orientalised' versions of designs by Matthias Lock and H. Copland in *A New Book of Ornaments* (1752). The doorcases appear to be made up from elements borrowed from engravings showing chimneypieces and mirrors in the same publication.

LATER DECORATION AND FURNISHINGS

The room has always been known as the Chinese Room and in the 1783 sale of Lord Verney's effects contained 'six mahogany Pembroke elbow chairs with cane seats and leather cushions'. By the late nineteenth century it had degenerated into a store for curiosities, but in 1893 Sir Harry furnished it as a bedroom with 'Chinese stuff', and had the walls painted yellow. The nodding Chinese figures in the niches and the Cantonese bamboo seat furniture, all of c.1800, survive from his arrangement. The room was redecorated in yellow and pink in 1956–7. The present blue accurately reproduces the eighteenth-century wall colour found here.

THE PAPER ROOM

The three flat-roofed 'domes' in the compartmented ceiling of this room suggest that this was the third of the bedrooms on this floor – perhaps even that described as 'My Lord's Bed Chamber' in the 1784 sale catalogue. Its present name derives from a long period of use as a storeroom for the family papers, but it was probably the 'French

A carving depicting a Chinese tea ceremony inside the alcove

The Paper Room chimneypiece features a Gothic temple flanked by diminutive cottages

Room', the third of a triumvirate of what were described as 'lesser rooms ... furnished in all tastes, as the Chinese Room, the Gothic Room, the French Room, etc., but all bad', seen by a visitor to the unfinished house in 1768.

DECORATION

Lightfoot's carved woodwork survives only in part and includes the enrichments on the ceiling, the remains of a fretwork dado and the carved consoles which occur at widely spaced intervals around the cornice of the room – supposedly every other one was removed in 1862 to adorn the bookcases in the Library downstairs. The surrounds of the west-facing windows are richly carved, but those on the north wall – where the Rotunda stood until 1791 – are plain and crude in the extreme.

CHIMNEYPIECE

Perhaps the room's best surviving feature is its chimneypiece, a charming Rococo surround in carved wood bearing scenes on the frieze showing a triple-arched Gothic temple flanked by cottages with a plume of smoke issuing from their chimneys and suns beaming down upon them. A design attributed to Lightfoot for an overmantel with ho-ho birds perching amidst Rococo flourishes appears to be for this chimneypiece.

ARCHITECTURAL FRAGMENTS

The battered fragments of architecture and carved woodwork which have been assembled on the north wall of the room were rescued from out-houses and the cellars of the house. They are relics of lost decorations by Lightfoot, perhaps from the demolished portion of Earl Verney's great palace, and include a great door, richly applied with a mixture of Gothic and classical motifs, inlaid with holly and boxwood. This may be the remains of the 'fine door' between the Ballroom and Withdrawing Room, mentioned by Robinson in a letter of 20 August 1768 as being 'the same size and dementions of the entrance door'. It was probably never installed, as it bears no marks of hinges or door furniture. The caryatid figures seem to have once flanked doorcases, and, as similar, but less freakish, supporters were a feature of the domed interior of the Rotunda at Ranelagh, Lightfoot may have intended them for the Rotunda Hall at Claydon. Their bases now support the octagonal mosaic table in the Library.

DRAWINGS

The two largest framed architectural drawings hanging on the north wall are designs attributed to Sir Thomas Robinson showing the full extent of the west and south fronts of Claydon before the demolitions of 1791–2.

THE GARDEN AND PARK

The park at Claydon was formed between 1763 and 1776. In a letter to the 2nd Earl Verney dated 10 September 1768, Sir Thomas Robinson wrote proposing 'to bring down the *capability* Brown – at least to give an opinion on [the] intended piece of water – but I only mention this a wish, yr Ldp will do [as] you please'. But Brown never came to Claydon, and instead John Sanderson of Caversham, a land surveyor and nurseryman, was commissioned to lay out the grounds. He caused the three crescent-shaped lakes to be dug, 'very tastefully displayed so as to resemble a natural river', and imported shrubs and plants from Brussels. His charges for the work amounted in all to £3,399. The lakes were further extended in the nineteenth century, when the north-western arm and the island were created. Originally the main drive to the house led up to the west front, before which once stood an equestrian statue. The drive fell into disuse after the demolitions of 1791–2; the present terrace and ha-ha were formed in the late nineteenth century.

The principal ornamental feature of the garden – although Sanderson may not have considered it so at the time – is All Saints church, the ancient parish church of Middle Claydon, which perches, literally in the middle of the garden, on a hillock less than 50 metres from the house. Originally a graveyard lay between them, and it was the 2nd Earl who ordered its removal and replacement with lawn. The local populace regarded this act of desecration with horror, one which was bound to bring great misfortune on the family. According to one old lady, who told the story to Lady Parthenope Verney, 'He never prospered arter that, ye know, for why, he moved the dead. But they was all back again next marnin! Safe in their graves!'

The pleasure grounds lie before the south front and are reserved for the private use of the family.

The house and the church from the north-west

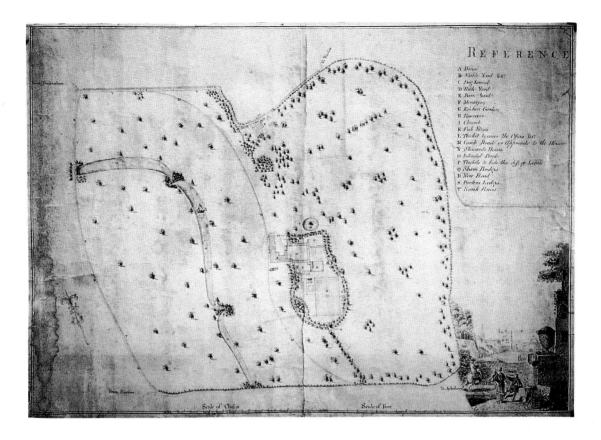

REFERENCE

A *House*
B *Stable Yard &c.*
C *Dog Kennel*
D *Rick Yard*
E *Barn Yards*
F *Menagery*
G *Kitchen Garden*
H *Reservoir*
I *Church*
K *Fish Stews*
L *Thicket to cover the Offices &c.*
M *Coach Road or Approach to the House*
N *Stewards House*
O *Intended Ponds*
P *Thickets to hide the cliff of Levels*
Q *Sheep Penlots*
R *New Road*
S *Porters Lodges*
T *Sunk Fences*

John Sanderson's scheme for remodelling the park

They contain excellent specimens of Cedar of Lebanon – including one reputedly planted from seeds brought back from Aleppo by John Verney in 1680 – and cypresses grown from seeds brought back from Vancouver by Edmund Verney in the 1860s.

THE CHURCH

The fourteenth-century church of All Saints is still the parish church of Middle Claydon and does not belong to the National Trust. However, it is of interest to the visitor as the resting place of the successive proprietors of Claydon and contains a number of good monuments. The earliest are a series of brasses to members of the Giffard family, who leased Claydon from the Verneys until 1620,

and the fine altar-tomb of Margaret Giffard with her alabaster effigy of 1539. The most notable of the Verney tombs is the imposing monument erected in 1653 by Sir Ralph Verney to his own memory and that of his wife, as well as his parents, Sir Edmund Verney and his wife Lady Margaret. Sir Ralph had commissioned a design for the tomb from an Italian artist while in Rome in 1652, but as executed, it was almost certainly designed by the sculptor Edward Marshall, who carved the beautiful busts which occupy the niches. The 2nd Earl Verney is buried in the crypt but has no monument and some of the later members of the family lie in the churchyard. Because of its uncomfortable proximity to the house, both Sir Ralph and the 2nd Earl Verney seriously considered demolishing the church, but family piety prevailed and the venerable edifice was extensively restored, at the expense of Sir Harry Verney, 2nd Bt, under the direction of Sir George Gilbert Scott in 1862.

35

CLAYDON AND THE VERNEYS

The Verneys have owned land in Buckinghamshire since the thirteenth century but have been the proprietors of Claydon only since *c.*1463, when the manor of Middle Claydon was purchased by Sir Ralph Verney, a merchant and sometime Lord Mayor of London. In 1478 he left it to his son, Sir John Verney, but neither Sir Ralph nor Sir John lived there, as they leased the estate to Roger Giffard, a kinsman, who built a manor house on the site of the present mansion. It was Giffard who erected the chancel of the church and is commemorated there by a fine brass to himself and his wife, Mary Verney. But by 1535 both church and house were reported to be in a decayed state, and a new lease, drawn up by Sir Ralph's great-grandson – also called Sir Ralph in the custom of the Verney family – stipulated that both must be repaired by the tenant, Sir Edward Giffard. In return for extending the lease from 80 to 100 years, Sir Ralph received a fine hunter valued at £30. The Verneys had lived at Pendley, near Ashridge in Hertfordshire, but this was sold by Sir Ralph's grandson, Sir Francis Verney, who realised what he could of his inheritance and left England to become a Barbary corsair. He died in 1616, aged 32 and without issue, miserably in a hospital in Messina. His young half-brother, Sir Edmund Verney, was compelled to redeem Claydon, purchasing it from the Giffard descendants in 1620 for £4,000, with fifteen years of the lease unexpired. Claydon was at this time a tall, red-brick, late Tudor house of H plan, bristling with pointed and crow-stepped gables, with balustraded galleries in the central bays of the north and south fronts. Although the Verneys had owned Claydon since about 1463, Sir Edmund was the first member of the family actually to reside there.

The north front of Claydon before the house was transformed by the 2nd Earl

SIR EDMUND VERNEY, 'THE STANDARD BEARER'

As a young man, Sir Edmund Verney served in the households of both James I's sons – first that of Henry, Prince of Wales, and then, after his premature death in 1612, his younger brother Charles, the future Charles I. In 1623 he accompanied Prince Charles and the Duke of Buckingham on their disastrous embassy to Madrid to woo the Spanish Infanta. On Charles's accession to the throne the following year, Verney was made Knight Marshal of the Palace and a Gentleman of the Privy Chamber. He was, according to the seventeenth-century historian David Lloyd: 'Of the strictness and piety of a Puritan, of the charity of a Papist, of the civility of an Englishman ... whose carriage was such that he was called "the only courtier that was not complained of".'

Although Sir Edmund sat as MP for Chipping Wycombe in both the Long and Short Parliaments and disapproved of Charles's arbitrary and unpopular policies, he remained staunchly loyal to his royal master as the country plunged into civil war. At the outbreak of the hostilities in 1642 he explained his position to Edward Hyde (later 1st Earl of Clarendon):

I do not like the Quarrel, and do heartily wish that the King would yield and consent to what they desire; so that my Conscience is only concerned in Honour and in Gratitude to follow my Master. I have eaten his Bread, and served him for nearly thirty Years, and will not do so base a Thing as to forsake him; and chuse rather to lose my Life (which I am sure I shall do) to preserve and defend those Things which are against my Conscience to preserve and defend. For I will deal freely with you, I have no Reverence for the Bishops for whom this Quarrel subsists.

Sir Edmund Verney,
'the Standard Bearer';
by Van Dyck
(Saloon)

Like so many families of the period, the Verneys had divided loyalties during the Civil War. While Sir Edmund remained with the King, his eldest son Ralph openly favoured the Parliamentary cause, and Edmund or 'Mun', the third son, threw his lot in with the Royalists and went to fight for them in Ireland. Despite their differing political allegiances, the touching letters which the Verneys continued to write to one another allow us an insight into the hopes and fears, as well as the daily activities, of a family during these troubled times. The letters are still preserved amongst the family papers at Claydon and have been published in *Memoirs of the*

Verney Family (1892–9), a minor classic of its kind.

In 1639, although already advanced in years, Sir Edmund was summoned to accompany the King on an expedition to suppress the rebellious Covenanters in Scotland. Ralph implored his father to keep out of trouble and send someone else in his place, but the old knight insisted on doing his duty. Sir Edmund stood by the King throughout the ensuing troubles and it is a measure of the trust in which he was held that, in August 1642, at the raising of the Royal Standard in Nottingham, he was made Bearer of the King's Standard. As he had foretold, Sir Edmund lost his

The Verney tomb in the church bears busts of the Standard Bearer (top left), his wife, Margaret (top right), with his son, Sir Ralph, and daughter-in-law, Mary

life defending his sovereign, at the Battle of Edgehill on 23 October 1642. One account tells how Sir Edmund had 'adventured' with the Royal Standard amongst the enemy so 'the souldiers might be encouraged to follow him. He was offered his life by a throng of his enemies, upon condition he would deliver the standard; he answered that his life was his own, but the standard was his and their sovereign's, and he would not deliver it while he lived.' Even in death he refused to relinquish his charge and they had to hack off the hand that grasped it. It is said that this hand was the only part of his body that was ever found, and the grisly relic is the sole occupant of his tomb in Claydon church. The ring which he wore on his finger, containing a miniature portrait of Charles I, is still piously preserved by the family. Thus died Sir Edmund Verney, 'The Standard Bearer', whom Clarendon described as 'a man of great courage and of a very cheerful and generous nature and confessedly valiant'.

John, 1st Viscount Fermanagh, who rebuilt the family fortunes (Pink Parlour)

SIR RALPH VERNEY, 1ST BT

Despite his espousal of the Parliamentarian cause, Sir Ralph Verney did not prosper during the Commonwealth. As conscientious and high-principled as his father, he refused to sign the Solemn League and Covenant and was forced to withdraw to Blois in France in 1643, 'preferring the miseries of exile to the soiling of his conscience'. As a result, he was expelled from the House of Commons, and Claydon and his other estates were sequestrated. When Hillesden, a neighbouring seat and the home of the Dentons, his mother's family, was burnt by Parliamentary soldiery early in 1644, there were rumours that Claydon would get the same treatment. After four years' absence, Lady Mary, Sir Ralph's wife, returned to find Claydon 'lamentably furnished … the feather beds that were waled up are much eaten with Ratts … spitts and other things are so extreamly eaten with Rust thatt they canot be evoir of any use againe … the dining-room chairs in Ragges'.

The sequestration order was eventually removed, but misfortune continued to dog the family: two of their infant children died in exile and in 1649 Ralph's brother Edmund, the lieutenant-colonel of the Royalist garrison defending Drogheda, was treacherously murdered after the town surrendered to the Parliamentary forces. Lady Verney herself died upon returning to Blois, but her body was reverently conveyed to Claydon and interred there in November 1650. After nine years of wandering, Sir Ralph returned to England in January 1653 – only to be confined for seventeen weeks on Cromwell's orders because 'he would not give recognisances to the Protector'. But the prospects for the family improved on the Restoration in 1660, when Sir Ralph was made a baronet. He re-entered Parliament, although thereafter he maintained at all times a sturdy independence from fashionable politics. Sir Ralph died at Claydon aged 83 in 1696 and lies beneath the great family tomb he commissioned for the church. With its marble busts commemorating himself and his

Ralph, 1st Earl Verney (Great Red Room)

However, the new Earldom was not to go to his eldest son, John, for he predeceased his father in 1737, but was instead inherited by his second son Ralph, and it is to him as 2nd Earl that we owe the transformation of Claydon into the house it is today.

THE 2ND EARL AND THE BUILDING OF CLAYDON

At the time of his succession in 1752, the 2nd Earl was an extremely wealthy man, for two good marriages had handsomely augmented the fortunes of the Verney family. In 1736 his elder brother John had married Mary Nicholson, the daughter of a London merchant who brought him £20,000, with a promise of a further sum on the death of her father. On John's premature death a year later, his wife's dowry, thanks to the inexorable laws of male descent, became the property of his brother Ralph, the heir to the Verney line and estates.

wife, as well as his parents, Sir Edmund and Lady Margaret, the monument constitutes a portrait gallery of the seventeenth-century proprietors of Claydon.

Sir Ralph's second son John, a London merchant, succeeded as 2nd Baronet, and greatly revived the fortunes of the family through his shrewd dealings with the Levant, African and East India companies, being created Viscount Fermanagh in 1703. In *The History and Antiquities of the County of Buckingham* (1847) George Lipscomb describes him as of 'countenance pale and ghastly; a large polypus descending from his right nostril', but despite his unappealing appearance Lord Fermanagh had three wives. It was he who first arranged the family papers at Claydon. His son Ralph, who succeeded in 1717, sat in Parliament as the MP for Wendover. 'Being unconcerned for any party' and voting consistently with the administration, he was rewarded by being made an Irish Earl by the Whigs in 1743.

Ralph, 2nd Earl Verney, the builder of the house

The carvings of birds over the door in the North Hall

Moreover, in 1740 Ralph had himself married an heiress, Mary Herring, a daughter of a governor of the Bank of England with £30,000 in cash, shares and land. Before succeeding to his inheritance, Ralph Verney had been a model heir, being a diligent student while at Cambridge and a conscientious steward of the family estates, carrying out improvements like the enclosure of East Claydon in 1741–2 and the planting of much new timber. There were no hints of the tendency towards the extravagance and love of display which were to lead to his downfall.

Between 1740 and 1767 the Verney estates had been greatly increased, as a considerable part of the wealth that had recently come into the family was expended on consolidating and extending their landholdings in Buckinghamshire. Therefore, it was only natural that the new Earl should want to rebuild the house to reflect the newly enhanced status of his family in the county. Although it had

been continually modernised and recast since the early seventeenth century, the venerable manor house at Claydon must have presented a run-down and unimpressive sight to eighteenth-century eyes. Verney's initial forays into building were modest enough: the handsome brick-built Stable Court was complete by 1754, and work was progressing on the east wing, likewise in red brick, in 1757. Then came the first instalment of the main house – the surviving block behind the west front, built of stone and containing the state rooms which were ready to receive their decorations by 1768. This part of the house was surely first conceived as a composition in its own right, with a front door in place of the present Venetian window. However, plans were soon underway to add a great Ballroom and a Rotunda, or Entrance Hall, to the north, making the executed wing merely a pavilion of an extended west front 256 feet long.

Another reason for Earl Verney's grandiose change of plan may have been to impress upon his neighbours his new-found role as a political power in the county. Verney had embarked upon a career in politics almost as soon as he had succeeded to his father's title, getting himself elected in the Liberal interest as MP for his father's old seat of Wendover in 1753 (being an Irish peer, he could sit in the English House of Commons). He represented Carmarthen in 1763, but retained Wendover as a pocket borough by nominating his protégé, Edmund Burke, for the seat. Through Burke, Verney sought to gain political influence, but paid handsomely for the privilege, lending the great orator £20,000 in one year alone. When Burke was ejected from Wendover at the 1768 election, Verney turned all his tenants in the town out of their houses and for six months forced them to live in tents 'in all the sorrow of penitence, until a promise of good behaviour in future softened the rigour of this nobleman's resentment as to suffer them all, with some few exceptions, to repossess their former dwellings'. In 1768, just before Verney embarked upon the final stage of his rebuilding of Claydon, he won one of the sought-after seats representing the county of Buckinghamshire. He was to hold it in unbroken succession until 1784. Moreover, Claydon was near Stowe, the palatial seat of his political rival Earl Temple, the most powerful of all Buckinghamshire magnates, and with the splendours of Stowe continually before him, there is little wonder that Earl Verney's plans for embellishing Claydon became ambitious.

In his grandiose undertaking at Claydon, Verney was doubtless egged on by Luke Lightfoot, the brilliant woodcarver who had been in charge of the building work on the house since 1757 and was responsible for the increasingly extravagant and freakish décors which were then appearing in the state rooms of the house. However, by 1768 Verney was perhaps tiring of Lightfoot's Rococo eccentricities and he called in Sir Thomas Robinson, a gentleman-architect of sound Palladian principles and his business partner in the Ranelagh pleasure gardens in London, to advise upon the house. Robinson thoroughly disapproved of Lightfoot, whom he once described as 'an *ignorant Knave*, with no small spice of *madness*

in his composition', and endeavoured to depose him, citing improprieties of taste, poor construction methods and evidence of dishonesty. But Lord Verney was reluctant to dismiss his protégé, and for a year the two men worked together at Claydon in an uneasy collaboration, with Robinson's plasterer Joseph Rose gradually taking over the decoration of the state rooms and Lightfoot becoming ever more sulky and uncooperative. His shoddy construction was already giving rise to grave concern, and in August 1769 Rose's plasterers, working in the Ballroom, 'fled for fear of the roof falling in'. Lightfoot was dismissed shortly afterwards. Robinson's description of their last interview conjures up a vivid picture of his vanquished enemy: 'He recd me in his parlour with his *Hat* on his head an *austere* look, fierce as an Eastern Monarch, his Eyes sparkl'd fire, his *Countenance* angry and revengeful, did not ask me to sit down.' Since much of Lightfoot's work for

Sir Thomas Robinson, the gentleman-architect who took over the rebuilding of Claydon from Lightfoot; by Frans van der Mijn (National Portrait Gallery)

The interior of the Rotunda at Ranelagh Gardens in London, in which Lord Verney was an investor. Painted by Antonio Canaletto (National Gallery, London)

Claydon remained in his Southwark workshop, Verney was urged to go there without delay and arrange to 'get every carving belonging to your Ldp pack'd or cased up, & the marbles unwrought to be taken from his Custody & sent to Claydon – you will have him in your power & he must give you the designs for finishing the work begun'.

It was only after Lightfoot's departure that the full scale of his deceptions was revealed. The matter was pursued in the Chancery case Verney v. Lightfoot, which came before the Lord Chancellor in 1771. Lord Verney asserted that he had supplied Lightfoot with £30,000 worth of money and materials, but had only ever received £7,000 worth of work or goods in return. Lightfoot was arrested but was allowed bail and eventually agreed to compensate his former patron by assigning to him £6,200 worth of property and business interests. In later life Lightfoot set up a victualling

business on Denmark Hill, near Dulwich – in a large property doubtless purchased with the proceeds of his misappropriations – where he died in 1789. His son Theophilus Lightfoot appears to have emigrated to Australia where his descendants still live, using, curiously enough, the name 'Verney' as a Christian name in each generation. Robinson had himself quarrelled with Verney in 1771, and the work of completing the Rotunda and Ballroom continued under the direction of William Donn, but was hampered by Earl Verney's worsening financial problems. The Italian *stuccatore* Bernato Bernasconi was working on the decorative plasterwork of the Ballroom right up until the crisis of 1784, but the artist G. B. Colomba was still pursuing payment for 88 painted panels for the Hall in 1791.

Verney's expensive building works may have contributed towards his financial downfall in 1784, and his personal extravagance cannot have helped. Lipscomb asserts that in his years of prosperity the 2nd Earl was invariably attended by 'a brace of tall negroes with silver French-horns behind his coach and six, perpetually making a noise like Sir Henry Sidney's "trompeters" in the days of Elizabeth, "blowing very joyfully to behold and see".' But it was his childlike unworldliness in business ventures that was chiefly responsible. Edmund Burke said of his old patron: 'It is past all description, past all conception, the supineness neglect and blind security of my friend in everything that concerns him. He suspects nothing, fears nothing, he takes no precautions, he imagines all mankind to be his friend' – as Burke knew well, for he and his cousin William owed Verney £71,000 between them by 1784 – a debt they never repaid. The Burkes' debts were partly political expenses, for then, as now, electioneering was a notoriously costly pursuit. Earl Verney's openhanded generosity in his own campaigns must have cost him vast sums, but he clung tenaciously on to his seat in Parliament, partly because it gave him immunity from arrest for debt.

Verney's lavish patronage was extended to others, not only indigent poets like Robert Bloomfield or impoverished clergymen like his old friend, the Rev. Samuel Rogers, but also the promoters of risky or fraudulent ventures. In the early 1760s Verney was enticed by Lightfoot into a joint speculation to build houses in London which quickly led to litigation, and he also lost his investment in the pleasure gardens at Ranelagh. Then there was the English Linen Company, which has been described as 'one of the most audacious smuggling projects of the century', a scheme for extracting 'metal, coal and sulphur' from wastelands near Pontefract in Yorkshire, and a Cornish tin mine, both of which turned out to be failures. It later emerged that Verney was often the only shareholder to have paid for his shares in advance. However, these losses were minute when compared with the £70,000 he lost in the crash of the Dutch East India Company in 1769. His Amsterdam brokers sued for the entire sum, and in 1771 Verney was ordered to pay off the debt in annual instalments of £5,000, depriving him of more than half his annual income. This placed a crippling burden on his already encumbered resources, and the Earl resorted to desperate measures to extricate himself from his debts, refusing to acknowledge them, discounting bills and notes of hand, raising loans and mortgages on his estates and selling family annuities. In 1774 Lady Verney assigned to her husband the money left to her privately by her father's will, and they sold silver in 1776, diamonds and plate in 1781 and 1782.

By 1775 Verney had a full-time lawyer to manage his debts, and in 1781 he hired a sinister individual named John MacNamara, who took over the management of the Earl's affairs on behalf of his trustees. In return the Earl was to receive an assured income of £2,000 a year. But MacNamara came to dominate Verney, inviting him down to Claydon as a guest and only allowing him to use the house on payment of £400 a year. It was he who forced the sales of the rich furnishings of both Claydon and the London house by Christie's in 1783 and 1784. Despite these measures, Verney's financial situation continued to deteriorate, and MacNamara took to writing his employer threatening letters and exploiting his estates still further to recoup the losses. In 1784, after losing his Parliamentary seat in the election, Verney was obliged to escape to France to avoid being arrested for debt.

From 1786, under the terms of a new trust formed after MacNamara had been dismissed, Verney's affairs were gradually put on to a more secure footing and he was able to return from exile. The Earl's few remaining years were spent under the strict supervision of his trustees, and it was with great reluctance that they permitted him to stand again for his Buckinghamshire county seat in the election of 1790. When Verney was returned, an election breakfast was held at Claydon for 200 gentlemen to celebrate the result – this being perhaps the only occasion the Earl ever used his great house for the purpose he intended. But for most of this period Claydon was shuttered and empty, and there is a pathetic story recounted by Christopher Hussey in *Country Life*, of how 'shortly before the Earl's death in 1791, a lad about the deserted stable at Claydon looked in at one of the cobwebbed windows of the great empty house and saw his broken master passing through the fantastic, derelict halls of his creation, to which he had been secretly brought for a last sight'. The 2nd Earl Verney died in London in 1791, at the age of 78.

THE NINETEENTH AND TWENTIETH CENTURIES

Lord Verney was succeeded by his niece Mary, the posthumous child of his elder brother John, who immediately set about putting her inheritance in order. Most of the land bought by her uncle was sold and the proceeds used to pay off the outstanding claims on the estate. In November 1791 she began pulling down his grandiose Ballroom and Rotunda, an undertaking that took almost a year to accomplish, retaining the southern portion of the house intact as the centrepiece of the Verney domains – although she herself rarely went there, preferring to reside in a villa in Kent. In 1792 Mary Verney reluctantly accepted the title of Baroness Fermanagh, but the title died with her,

Mary, Baroness Fermanagh, who demolished most of the 2nd Earl's house (Library)

for she never married, and died in 1810, the last of her ancient race. Her portrait, variously described as 'kindly but shrewd' and 'of prim and disapproving countenance', hangs in the Library.

In her will Lady Fermanagh bequeathed Claydon and its estate to her uterine half sister, Catherine Calvert, with whom she had been brought up, their mother having remarried a Mr Richard Calvert of Bexley in Kent. Catherine and her husband, the Rev. Robert Wright, Rector of Middle Claydon, assumed the name of Verney in accordance with Lady Fermanagh's wishes, and lived in what remained of the house. But they had no children, and on Catherine's death in 1827 she left Claydon to Harry Calvert, the son of Sir Harry Calvert, 1st Bt, her first cousin once removed.

Sir Harry, the 2nd Baronet, resigned his commission in the Grenadier Guards at the age of 23 and set out to travel the world. He developed appendicitis in mid-Atlantic and was put ashore at Bahia in Brazil to die. Instead he recovered and rode across the Andes, meeting and making friends with the South American revolutionary Simon Bolivar on his way to Santiago. He later visited Java and Singapore before returning to take up his inheritance at Claydon in 1827, changing his name from Calvert to Verney. He proved to be a conscientious and effective landlord, rebuilding the cottages of his tenantry and initiating many agricultural improvements on the estate. He also represented Buckingham in Parliament for many years and was a founding member of the Royal Agricultural Society of England and of the Red Cross.

Sir Harry married twice, his second wife being Frances Parthenope, the eldest daughter of William Nightingale of Embley, Hampshire, and sister of Florence Nightingale. The Nightingale sisters had been born in Italy and were named after the places of their birth, Parthenope being the Greek name for Naples. Florence Nightingale often stayed at Claydon, and her room, together with many relics connected with her, is still reverently preserved at Claydon today. Sir Harry was devoted to his sister-in-law and was affectionately known in Parliament as the 'Member for Florence Nightingale'.

Sir Harry Verney with his sister-in-law, Florence Nightingale

Sir Harry and Parthenope loved Claydon and did much to revive the house after its long period of neglect. Parts of the fabric were found to be in a perilous condition – doubtless a legacy of Lightfoot's amateurish construction methods. They carried out extensive repairs and alterations in 1859–62, recasting the south front and the east-wing in the Jacobean taste to make it 'more agreeable and convenient to live in', and establishing the present entrance on the north front. The alter-

ations were carried out by John Burlison from the office of Sir George Gilbert Scott, who also supervised the thorough restoration of the parish church. The Verneys were evangelical Anglicans and were noted for their piety as well as for their support of liberal causes. It was Parthenope who sorted the family papers and edited the first two volumes of *Memoirs of the Verney Family*. The house was also refurnished during their time, as, excepting the family portraits, it had been virtually emptied by MacNamara's sales. Old photographs show the eclectic displays of military and ethnographic trophies that Sir Harry devised amidst the Rococo glories of Lightfoot's carved woodwork.

Many of Sir Harry's trophies had been obtained by his eldest son, Edmund Hope Verney, who entered the Royal Navy at the age of twelve in 1851 and subsequently served in the Crimea and in India during the Mutiny. In 1862 he was posted to Vancouver Island in Canada to take command of the *Grappler*, and there formed an important collection of native artefacts, some of which are now in the British Museum. He succeeded as the 3rd Baronet in 1894, but died in 1910. His widow,

Margaret, Lady Verney on the staircase at Claydon; by Sir William Blake Richmond, 1869 (Pink Parlour)

Margaret, continued a tradition established by Parthenope by editing further volumes of *Memoirs of the Verney Family*. She also published Sir Thomas Robinson's correspondence with the 2nd Earl discussing the building of the house. The letters had been discovered by her daughter-in-law, Lady Rachel Verney, amongst the Claydon muniments and revealed much about the authorship of the house, which had hitherto always been ascribed to Robert Adam.

The 4th Baronet, Sir Harry Calvert Williams Verney, continued the family tradition of military service followed by Parliamentary duties as MP for North Buckinghamshire between 1910 and 1918. He and his son Ralph, the 5th Baronet, gave the house and restrictive covenants over 392 acres of the park to the National Trust in 1956. Most of the contents of Claydon still belong to the Verney family, and in 1987 Sir Ralph established the Claydon House Trust to safeguard the family portraits and papers and ensure that they always remain in the house. In 1996 21.2 hectares (52 acres) of parkland were transferred to the National Trust to preserve the setting of the house. The estate is now farmed by Sir Edmund Verney, Sir Ralph's son who inherited the Verney baronetcy in 2001, and now lives in the east wing with his family.

The National Trust, assisted by a grant from the Historic Buildings Council, carried out extensive repairs to the house in 1957. Further repairs were undertaken, again with help from the HBC, in 1973–7, when the house was redecorated, on the advice of John Fowler, through the generosity of an anonymous benefactor, and additional structural work was carried out to the house in 1992–4, supported by a grant from English Heritage.

SHORT BIBLIOGRAPHY

BOYNTON, Lindsay, 'Luke Lightfoot (?1722–1789)', *Furniture History*, ii, 1966, pp. 7–17.

HUSSEY, Christopher, 'Claydon House', *Country Life*, cxii, 24, 31 October, 7 November 1952, pp. 1278–81, 1398–1401, 1480–4.

HUSSEY, Christopher, *English Country Houses: Early Georgian*, 1965, p. 244 ff.

LEES-MILNE, James, *Claydon House, Buckinghamshire* (National Trust guidebook), 1961, revised by Gervase Jackson-Stops, 1978, revised by Christopher Wall and Jonathan Marsden, 1984, revised by Jonathan Marsden, 1995.

LIPSCOMB, George, *The History and Antiquities of the County of Buckingham*, i, 1847, pp. 186–8.

PRITCHARD, Allan, *Vancouver Island Letters of Edmund Hope Verney 1862–65*, 1996.

SHEAHAN, James Joseph, *History and Topography of Buckinghamshire*, 1862, pp. 358–65.

STONE, Lawrence, 'The Verney Tomb at Middle Claydon', *Records of Buckinghamshire*, xvi, 1953–60, pp. 67–82.

VERNEY, Lady [F.P], 'Claydon House', *Records of Buckinghamshire*, v, 1878, pp. 419–27.

VERNEY, Frances Parthenope and VERNEY, Margaret M. ed., *Memoirs of the Verney Family*, 4 vols., 1892–9.

VERNEY, Margaret, Lady and ABERCROMBIE, Patrick, 'Letters of an Eighteenth Century Architect', *Architectural Review*, lix, June 1926, pp. 258–63; lx, July–September 1926, pp. 1–3, 50–3, 92–3.

VERNEY, Margaret, Lady, ed., *Verney Letters of the Eighteenth Century*, 2 vols., 1930.

VERNEY, Peter, *The Standard Bearer: The Story of Sir Edmund Verney*, 1963.

WEAVER, Sir Lawrence, 'Claydon House', *Country Life*, xxxi, 9, 16 March 1912, pp. 356–64, 394–402.

WORSLEY, Giles, '"I thought myself in Paradise": Ranelagh Gardens and its Rotunda', *Country Life*, 15 May 1986, pp. 1380–4.

'Athena', Florence Nightingale's pet owl. Discovered while a chick fallen from its nest under the walls of the Acropolis in Athens in 1850 and brought back to England, the bird was tamed and became her pet. It died on the eve of her departure for the Crimea in 1854 (Miss Nightingale's Room)